for boring only aloud for 2 weeks

Fun to Learn PICTURE DICTIONARY

Illustrated by
Peter Harris

Designed and produced by
Autumn Publishing Ltd.
Chichester, West Sussex

© 2000 Autumn Publishing Ltd

Printed in Spain

ISBN 1 85997 433 3

A a

abacus

An **abacus** is an early form of calculator that was first used thousands of years ago. It has a wooden frame with rows of beads.

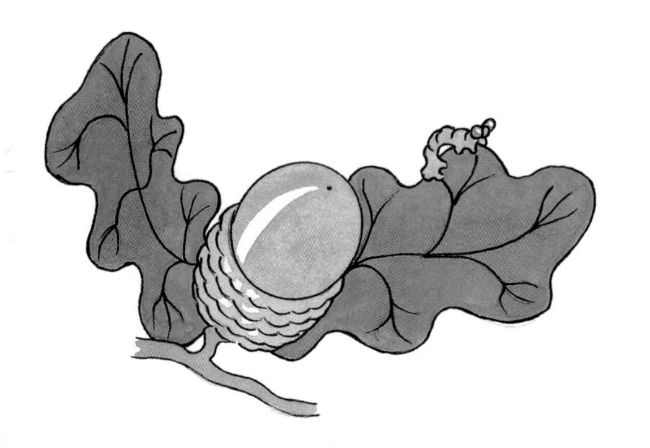

acorn

An **acorn** is the fruit and seed of the oak tree. An acorn is a smooth nut contained in a cup-shaped shell.

aeroplane

An **aeroplane** is a very powerful vehicle that can fly through the air.

alligator

An **alligator** is a reptile with a large mouth and many teeth, a long tail, and thick waterproof skin. Alligators always live close to water.

ambulance

An **ambulance** is a vehicle used in emergencies to take sick and injured people to hospital. It has a loud siren to warn other vehicles to clear the way.

animal

An **animal** is any living creature which can move by itself. For example, people, fish and birds are all animals, but trees and flowers are not.

ant

An **ant** is a small insect. Ants live in large groups, called colonies. Ants are found all over the world and can vary in size from 1mm to 4cm.

aquarium

An **aquarium** is a building or tank where water animals and plants are kept. Some people keep fish in small aquariums in their homes.

artist

An **artist** is someone who paints or draws pictures, or creates other kinds of art. Creative people are known as being artistic. You can see the work of artists in art galleries and museums.

astronaut

An **astronaut** is a person who is trained to fly a spacecraft. Astronauts make amazing discoveries about space and some have even walked on the Moon.

athlete

An **athlete** is a person who is very fit, healthy and good at sport. The best athletes from around the world compete in the Olympic Games.

avenue

An **avenue** is a wide street or road usually lined on both sides with trees.

B b

baby

A **baby** is a newly-born or very young child.

ballet

Ballet is a style of dance that tells a story when it is set to music. Male and female ballet dancers train and practise very hard to learn difficult ballet steps and movements.

balloons

Balloons are made of thin, coloured rubber. We blow into balloons to fill them with air.

A **balloon** is a large bag filled with hot air or gas. It has a basket fixed underneath which people can ride in.

banana

A **banana** is a long, sweet fruit with a yellow skin that you peel off. Bananas grow on banana plants in countries with hot climates.

barbecue

A **barbecue** is a meal cooked outdoors on an open fire. It is also the name given to the metal grill on which the food is cooked.

beach

A **beach** is the land by the edge of the sea. It is usually sandy or covered with small stones.

bear

A **bear** is a large, wild animal with thick fur. Bears can be brown or white depending on where they live. Brown bears usually live in woods and white bears live in the Arctic.

bedroom

A **bedroom** is a place where you sleep and sometimes play.

bicycle

A **bicycle** is a vehicle you can ride that has two wheels and pedals. You push on the pedals to make the wheels go round.

birthday

Your **birthday** is the day when you were born. In many countries children are given presents and cards on their birthday each year. Some people celebrate their birthday by having a party.

blizzard

A bad snow storm with strong winds is called a **blizzard**. Blizzards happen when the temperature falls below freezing.

blossom

The flowers that appear on trees in spring are called **blossom**. When blossom falls, fruit begins to grow.

boomerang

A **boomerang** is a thin, curved stick. Because of its shape, a boomerang will come back to the person who throws it. The boomerang originally came from Australia.

bridge

A **bridge** is a road or railway which crosses over something, such as a river or another road. Bridges can be built of steel, wood, bricks or concrete.

butterfly

A **butterfly** is an insect with large, sometimes brightly coloured, wings. Butterflies' wings help them to blend with their surroundings or to warn off other creatures.

C c

calculator

A **calculator** is a small machine which you use to solve maths problems. You can work out sums very quickly on a calculator.

calendar

A **calendar** shows the days, weeks and months of a year. You use calendars to remind you about important dates and events.

camera

A **camera** is a piece of equipment used for taking photographs. Cameras put still pictures onto film to make photographs.

Video cameras put moving pictures onto film to make programmes, films and home videos.

canoe

A **canoe** is a light narrow boat. It has no engine, and paddles are used to make it move.

cartoon

Cartoons are often found in comics, newspapers and magazines. The cartoon style of drawing makes things look funny.

Cartoons can also be made into animated films. There are many well-known cartoon characters.

caterpillar

A **caterpillar** is a small creature with a long body and many legs. Caterpillars turn into butterflies or moths.

cheese

Cheese is made from cow's or goat's milk and is good to eat. There are many different kinds of cheese from all around the world.

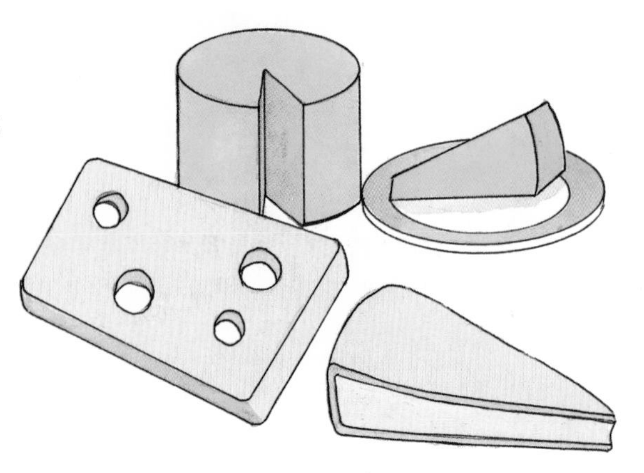

chimpanzee

A **chimpanzee** is an ape with long arms and no tail. Chimpanzees can be found in the forests of Africa. They are very intelligent animals and can use tools to help them find and eat certain foods. Chimpanzees can also learn to communicate with humans.

chocolate

A sweet food made from cocoa and sugar is called **chocolate**. Many popular snacks are made from, or coated with, chocolate.

clarinet

A **clarinet** is a long, thin musical instrument with keys. To make sounds you blow into a clarinet and press the keys with your fingers. Clarinets are woodwind instruments and make up part of an orchestra.

clock

A **clock** is a machine which tells you the time. The hours and minutes are shown by hands or numbers on the clock face. Alarm clocks can be set to ring or buzz to wake you up.

clown

A **clown** is a person who wears funny clothes and make-up. Clowns usually work in circuses, and make people laugh. They also sometimes entertain children at parties.

comet

A **comet** is a ball of ice and dust which travels around the solar system. This journey can take from three years to a million years. Comets can sometimes be seen travelling in the night sky.

compass

A **compass** is an instrument that people use to show which direction to travel. The four points of a compass are North, South, East and West. The arrow on a compass always points to North.

countryside

The **countryside** is the land away from towns where there are fields, woods, farms, lakes and villages.

D d

daffodil

A **daffodil** is a yellow flower which blooms in the spring. The middle part of the flower is shaped like a trumpet. The daffodil is the national flower of Wales.

dairy

A **dairy** is a place where milk is made safe for us to drink. Yoghurt, butter, cream and cheese are also made in a dairy.

dentist

A **dentist** is a person who takes care of your teeth, gums and jaws. Dentists treat any problems in your mouth.

If a hole appears in a tooth this should be treated by a dentist.

desert

A **desert** is a very hot and dry place. Only a few animals and plants can survive in a desert. Deserts are found in countries which are nearest to the sun.

dessert

A **dessert** is a sweet food usually eaten after lunch or dinner. You eat a dessert with a dessertspoon.

diary

A **diary** is a book where you write the things that happen to you each day. You can also use a diary to keep track of important dates and events. Some famous people from the past have kept diaries which tell us about the time when they lived.

dictionary

A **dictionary** is a book where you can find out how to spell words, and what they mean. Some dictionaries, like this one, have pictures to make them fun.

dinosaur

Dinosaurs were creatures that lived millions of years ago on land and in water. Some dinosaurs were harmless and fed on plants, but some hunted and fed on other dinosaurs.

doctor

A **doctor** is the person you go to see at a hospital, or surgery, when you are sick or injured. He or she will help you to get better.

dog

There are many different breeds of **dog**. Most are kept as pets, but some are trained to work, such as guide dogs, sheep dogs and police dogs.

dolphin

A **dolphin** is a mammal which lives in the sea. Dolphins are playful creatures and talk to each other by making a series of clicking noises.

dove

A **dove** is a bird which is usually grey or white and looks like a small pigeon. Doves make a cooing sound. The white dove is known as the dove of peace.

dragon

A **dragon** is a mythical monster that exists only in stories. It has wings and breathes fire.

dream

A **dream** is a picture or event seen through the mind of a person who is asleep.

dungeon

A long time ago a **dungeon** was a place under a building, such as a castle, where prisoners were kept.

E e

eagle

There are different types of **eagle**. One of the largest is the bald eagle which can have a wingspan of 2 – 2.5 metres. Eagles live in mountainous areas. They can soar high in the sky and glide without beating their wings.

ears

You use your **ears** to hear. Unlike people, many animals can move their ears in different directions to detect danger.

elephant

An **elephant** is a very large and strong animal. It is grey and has a long nose called a trunk. Elephants are found in Africa and India. Indian elephants are easier to train. They sometimes work in forests, moving logs.

emu

An **emu** is a large bird with shaggy feathers that lives in Australia. Emus cannot fly but have very strong, long legs which means they can walk long distances. Emus are related to the ostrich and kiwi which are also flightless birds.

encyclopedia

An **encyclopedia** is a large book or set of books. It is in alphabetical order and describes lots of different subjects.

envelope

When you write a letter and want to send it to someone you put it in an **envelope**.

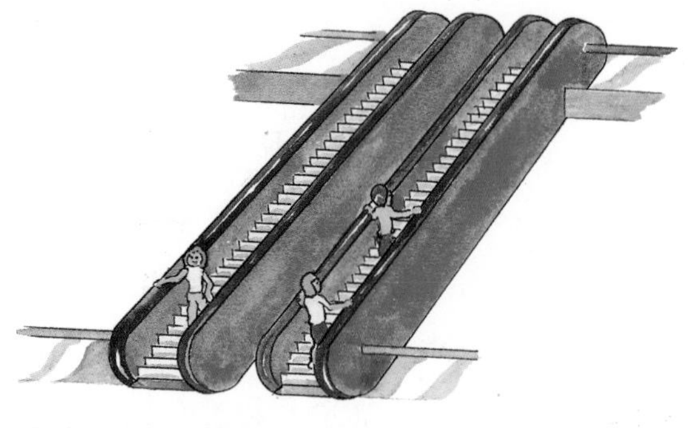

escalator

An **escalator** is a moving staircase. Escalators carry people up or down from one floor to another.

explorer

An **explorer** is a person who travels around the world learning about different countries and places.

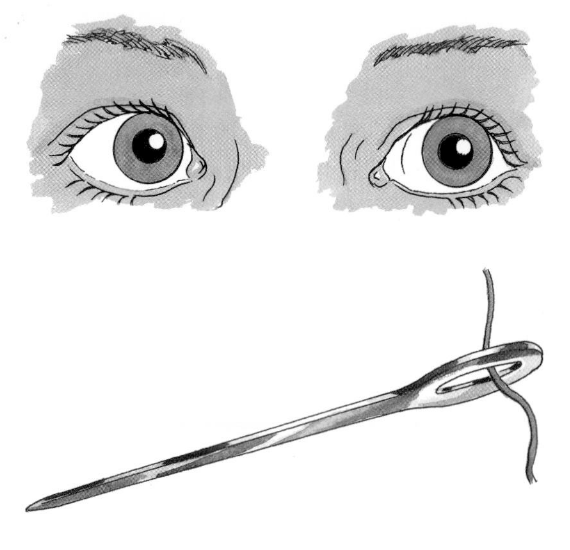

eyes

Eyes are the part of the face used for seeing. Eyelashes and eyebrows protect the eyes from dust and infection.

The small hole in a needle where thread goes through is called the **eye**.

F f

farm

A **farm** is land where crops are grown and animals are kept. Farms can be different sizes, from a few acres to hundreds of acres of land.

feathers

Feathers are the soft covering which keep birds warm. Feathers have a hollow stem which is covered with fine strands.

ferry

A **ferry** is a boat or ship that takes people from one side of a stretch of water to the other. Some ferries are big enough to carry cars and lorries, as well as people.

fish

A **fish** is any animal with scales and fins that lives and breathes under water.

flag

A **flag** is a piece of material with a pattern on it. Flags are used for many different occasions. Every country has its own flag.

flamingo

A **flamingo** is a bird with very long legs, a long neck and pink feathers. Flamingos live in shallow, salty lagoons and lakes. Their long legs enable them to wade into deeper water whilst using their long necks and beaks to reach for food.

foal

A **foal** is a baby horse or pony. The name for a male foal is colt and a female foal is a filly. Foals feed on their mothers' milk until they can eat grass.

football

Football is a game played by two teams of 11 players. The game is played on a grass pitch with a goal at each end and the aim is to kick the ball into the goal.

fork

Forks are different sizes and are used for different things. They have three or four points called prongs or tines. Small forks are used to pick up food. Larger forks with a long handle are used to dig gardens.

freckles

Freckles are small, brown or orange marks on the skin. Some people get freckles on their face when they have been in the sun.

friends

A friend is someone who you enjoy being with and someone who likes being with you. A friend is a person who will help you and be kind to you.

fruit

Fruit is the fleshy and juicy part of a plant with a seed. Some fruits are good to eat.

G g

galaxy

A **galaxy** is a large collection of stars grouped together in space. Earth is part of a galaxy called the Milky Way.

garden

A **garden** is a piece of ground around, or sometimes behind, a house. Flowers, fruit, and vegetables can be grown there. It can also be a place where you play.

giant

A **giant** is an imaginary person or creature who is very tall and large. Some animals are called giants, such as giant pandas and giant whales.

giraffe

A **giraffe** is an animal with a long neck and legs. Giraffes live in the open grasslands of Africa and eat leaves from tall trees. Giraffes are the tallest creatures in the animal kingdom.

glider

A **glider** is an aircraft without an engine. Gliders have very long wings to catch the wind. To get airborne they are towed by another aircraft and then released.

globe

A **globe** is a ball with a map of the world on it. Globes are usually on stands and you can spin them around. Globes are very interesting to look at to find out where different countries are in the world.

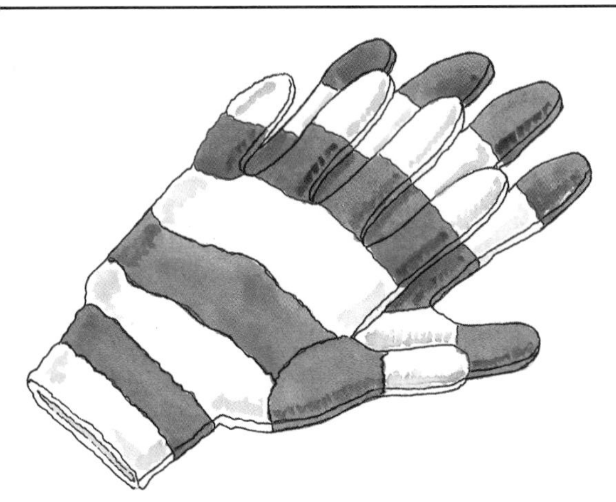

gloves

Gloves cover your hands. They have separate parts for fingers and thumbs. Gloves are worn to protect your hands and to keep them warm in winter.

gold

Gold is found in rocks and is a very expensive metal. Gold is a shiny, yellow metal and is used mostly to make jewellery.

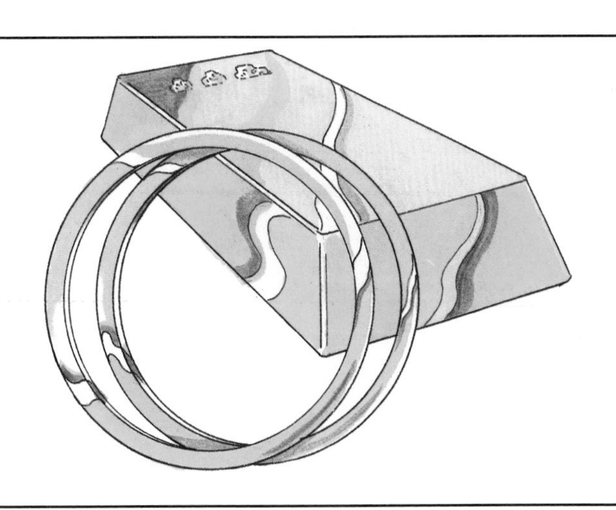

gooseberry

A **gooseberry** is a small, green fruit. It grows on a thorny bush. Gooseberries are quite sour to eat raw so are often cooked with sugar and put into pies.

grasshopper

A **grasshopper** is a green insect with long, powerful back legs which help it to jump from place to place. Grasshoppers make a noise by rubbing their back legs against their wings.

guitar

A **guitar** is a musical instrument belonging to the string family. It has six or 12 strings. You strum the strings with your fingers to make musical notes.

H h

hair

The soft covering on the body, and especially the head, is called **hair**. The hair on your head grows longer than on the rest of your body.

hammock

A **hammock** is a kind of bed that can be hung up by rope at each end. It is usually made of strong fabric such as canvas.

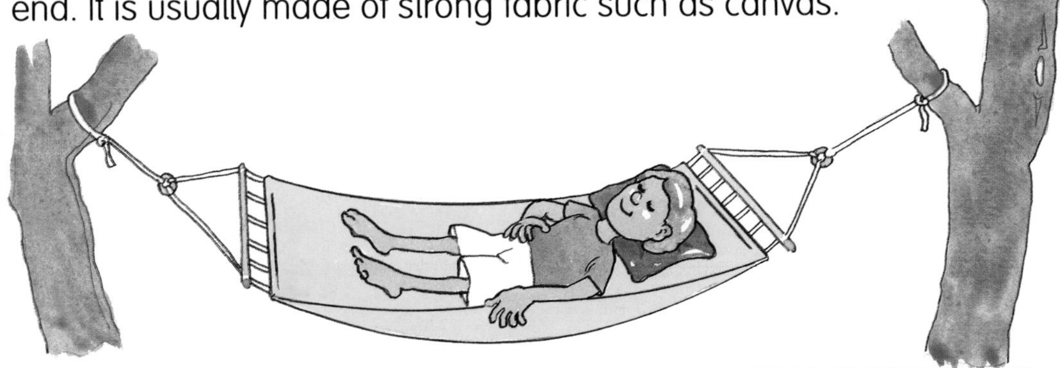

hamster

A **hamster** is a small, reddish-brown rodent. Golden hamsters are often kept as pets and originally came from Syria. Hamsters have cheek pouches where they store food such as grass and seeds.

harbour

A **harbour** is a place where boats, yachts and ships are kept when they are not at sea. It is also the place where goods are loaded onto ships and boats.

harp

A **harp** is a large, upright musical instrument belonging to the string family. Strings are stretched down a frame and played with the fingers. Harps are one of the oldest string instruments.

harvest

To **harvest** is to gather fruit, vegetables or corn when it is ripe.

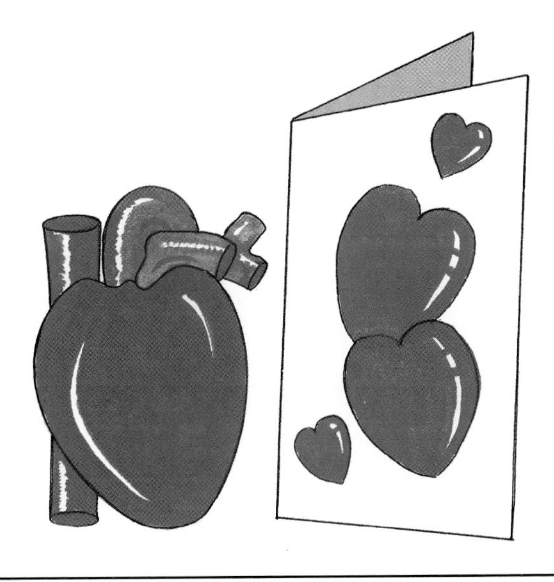

heart

The **heart** is the muscle inside your chest which pumps blood around your body. Every living animal has a heart.

A **heart** is also a shape that means love.

helicopter

A **helicopter** is an aircraft which can go straight up in the air. It has blades, called rotors, on its roof and tail.

helmet

A **helmet** is a special hard hat to protect the head. Some people, such as firemen, soldiers and cyclists, wear helmets for safety.

hill

A **hill** is part of the ground that is naturally higher than the land around it.

hippopotamus

A **hippopotamus** is a large, heavy animal which lives in Africa. Hippopotamuses spend most of their time in water and can sometimes stay under water for up to five minutes.

holly

The **holly** bush has shiny, green, prickly leaves and red berries. At Christmas time you use holly for decoration.

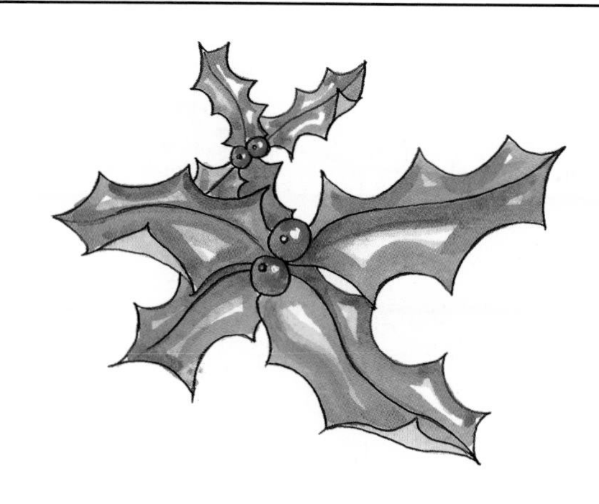

horse

A **horse** is a large, plant-eating animal that can be ridden. Some horses are used for sports such as racing and show-jumping. Some work as police horses, or are used for pulling carts.

hospital

A **hospital** is a place where people are looked after when they are too ill to be at home. Doctors and nurses look after people in hospital.

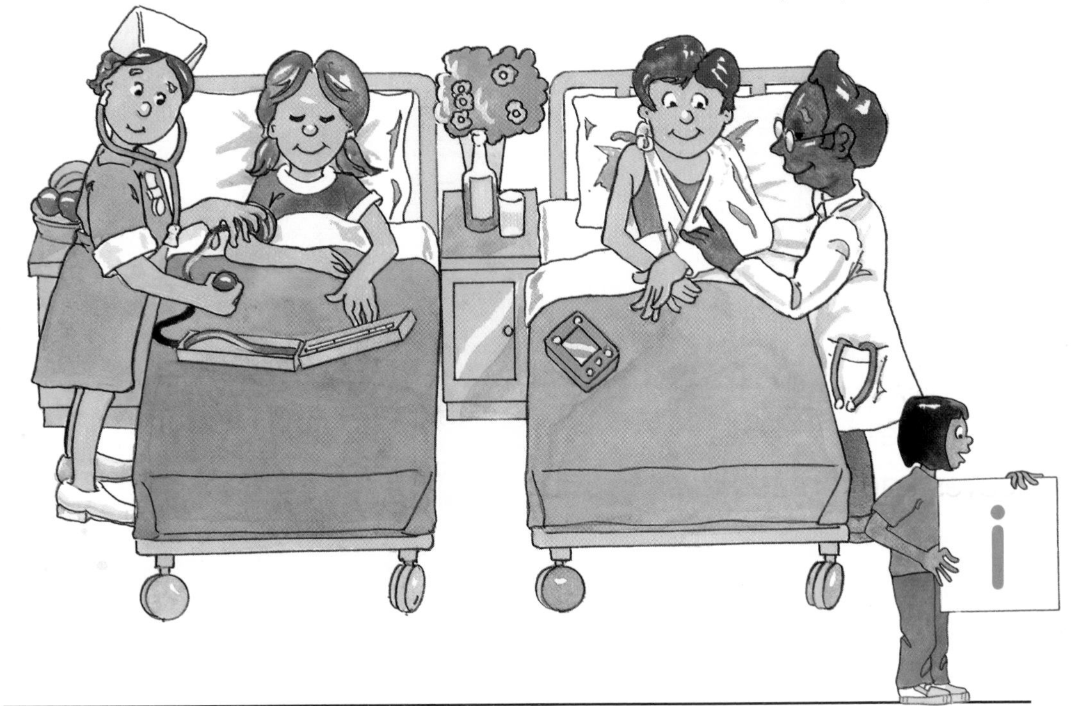

I i

ice-cream

Ice-cream is a very cold, sweet food that people usually eat when the weather is hot and sunny. You can buy ice-cream in many different flavours.

igloo

An **igloo** is a round house made from blocks of snow and ice. Many years ago the Inuit people lived in these houses.

ink

Ink is a coloured liquid used for writing and printing. Ink is used to print comics, magazines, newspapers and books.

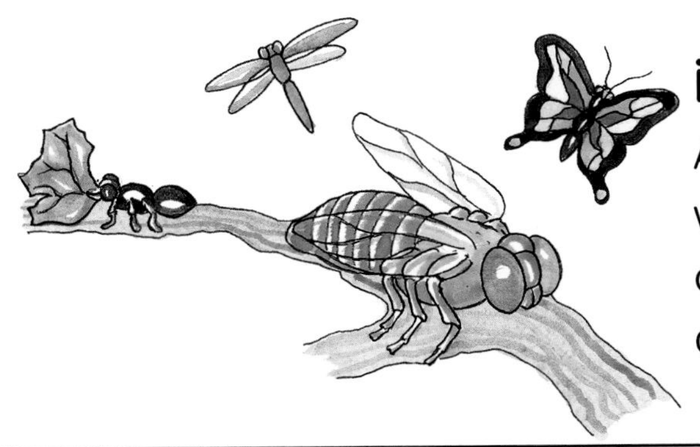

insect

An **insect** is a small creature with six legs. Flies, ants, dragonflies, wasps, bees and butterflies are insects.

instrument

An **instrument** is used to make music. There are many different types of musical instruments.

An **instrument** is sometimes another name for a tool.

island

An **island** is a piece of land that is completely surrounded by water.

J j

jacket

A **jacket** is a short, casual coat which you wear to keep warm. There are different types of jacket. A jacket can also be worn as part of a suit.

jelly

A sweet fruit dessert that wobbles when you move or touch it, is called **jelly**. You often have jelly and ice-cream at parties.

jewels

Jewels are precious and expensive stones. Jewels come in different colours and are used to decorate rings, earrings, bracelets and necklaces.

jockey

A **jockey** is a person who rides horses in races. Jockeys are usually very small and light so that the horses can run faster in races.

jungle

A **jungle** is full of trees, plants and wild animals. Jungles are in tropical areas where the climate is hot and steamy.

K k

kangaroo

Kangaroos live in herds in Australia. They have strong back legs and can jump for long distances. A female kangaroo has a pouch where she carries her young. A baby kangaroo is called a joey.

key

A **key** is a piece of metal used to open a lock.

A **key** is a small lever, or button, which is pressed with a finger. Pianos and computer keyboards have keys.

king

Some countries have royal families. The **king** is the head of a royal family and the ruler of his country.

kite

A **kite** is a frame covered with paper or thin material and attached to a long string. You can fly kites when it's windy and make them change direction by moving the strings.

knuckle

A **knuckle** is one of the pieces of bone at the top of your hand, between your fingers and your wrist.

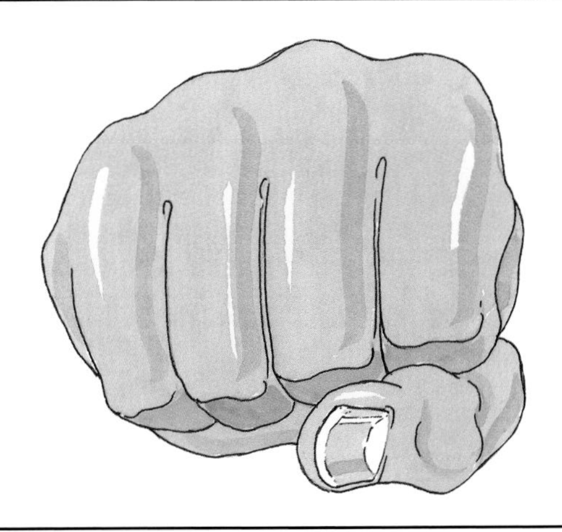

koala

A **koala** is a small, bear-like animal that lives in Australia. It spends most of its time eating the leaves of Eucalyptus trees. Koalas carry their young on their back.

L l

ladybird

A **ladybird** is a red or yellow flying insect, with spots on its wings.

lamb

A **lamb** is a baby sheep. Lambs are often born in the spring. They usually live on farms or high up in the hills or mountains.

lasso

A **lasso** is a long rope with a loop tied at one end. Cowboys in North America use lassos to help them catch cattle. A cowboy swings the lasso high in the air before throwing the loop over a stray cow.

leaf

A **leaf** is one of the flat green parts joined to the stem or branch of a tree or a plant.

lemon

A **lemon** is a yellow fruit with soft segments. Lemons taste sour which makes them difficult to eat raw. Lemons are used as a flavouring in food and drinks.

leopard

A **leopard** is a member of the cat family. Leopards have a golden coat covered with black spots, no two leopards have the same pattern of spots. These beautiful creatures live in the grasslands of Africa.

leotard

A **leotard** is a tight piece of clothing covering the torso and sometimes the arms and legs. Acrobats, gymnasts and ballet dancers wear leotards.

library

Libraries keep books on many different subjects. People can borrow books from the library to read. They can be taken home for a certain amount of time before they have to be returned.

lighthouse

A **lighthouse** is a tall building with a very powerful light at the top. The light flashes to guide ships or warn them of dangerous rocks.

lightning

Lightning is the flash of forked or jagged light that appears in the sky during a storm. Lightning often flashes just before thunder begins.

lips

Your **lips** are the outer part of your mouth. Together with your tongue and teeth, lips help you to form words and to eat and drink.

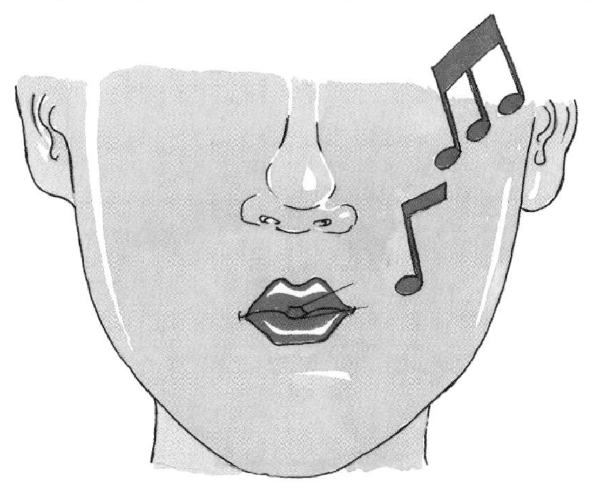

lobster

A **lobster** is a sea creature. It has a hard shell and two claws on its front legs, which it uses to catch food. Cooked lobster is good to eat.

M m

magician

A **magician** is a person who can do magic tricks. Magicians have to practise very hard to make their magic tricks believable.

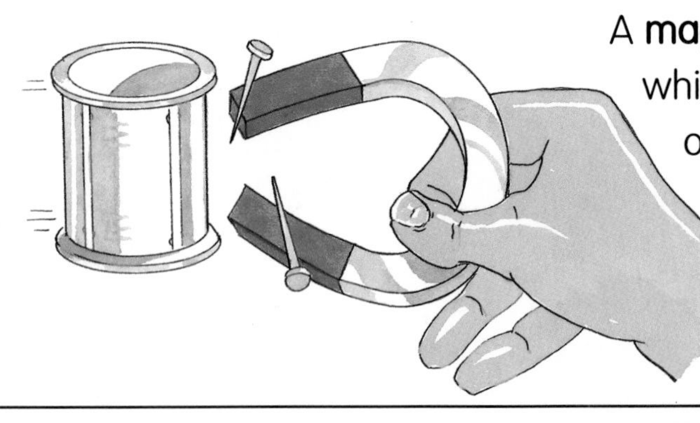

magnet

A **magnet** is a piece of metal which makes other pieces of metal stick to it. For instance, a magnet is very useful to pick up pins or nails.

magnifying glass

When you look through a **magnifying glass** it makes things appear bigger than they really are. This happens because the glass is curved.

map

A **map** is a diagram that shows where different places in the world are. Maps can also be of towns and show the streets to help you find your way around.

mask

A **mask** is something put over the face to hide it. Masks can be worn for fun at parties. Many people such as builders, doctors and dentists have to wear masks for protection whilst they are working.

maze

A **maze** is a set of paths and hedges that twist and turn. They are a type of puzzle where you have fun trying to find your way out.

medal

A **medal** is a metal disc joined to coloured ribbon. People are given medals when they have done something exceptionally skilful or brave, such as winning a race or helping someone in danger.

medicine

If you are ill your doctor will give or prescribe **medicine** to make you feel better. Medicines are usually taken by mouth as a liquid or pill.

mermaid

A **mermaid** is a storybook creature that is half woman and half fish. In stories and myths mermaids live under the sea.

microphone

A **microphone** is a piece of electrical equipment that you can speak or sing into to make your voice sound louder. Microphones are also used in tape recorders, hearing aids and radio and television broadcasts.

mirror

A **mirror** is a piece of glass where you can see your reflection. Mirrors can be small and held in your hand or fixed to a wall or dressing table.

moon

The **Moon** is the natural satellite that moves around the Earth. You can see the Moon at night when it shines in the sky.

motorcycle

A **motorcycle** is a vehicle that has two wheels. It has a large engine to make it go very fast.

mountains

Mountains are areas of land which rise to a great height. There are some very well-known mountain ranges such as the Alps in Europe, the Himalayas in Asia and the Rocky Mountains in the United States of America.

music

Music is the sound created by people singing. Music is also made by musical instruments being played, or both singing and playing together.

n

N n

nail

Your **nail** is the hard part that grows on your fingers and toes.

A **nail** is a sharp, pointed piece of metal. It is hammered into pieces of wood to hold them together.

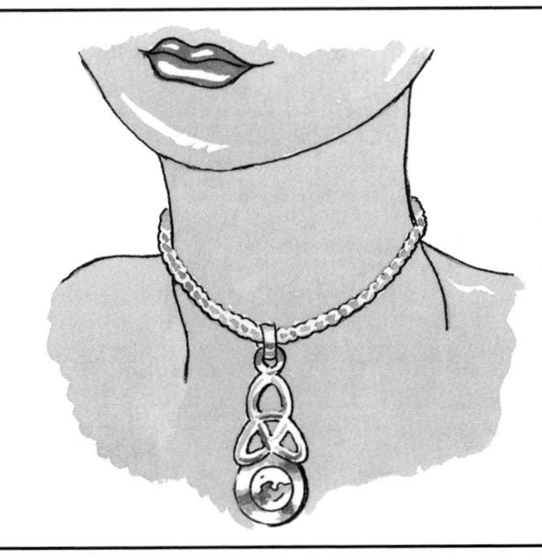

necklace

A **necklace** is a piece of jewellery that is worn around the neck. Necklaces can be a string of beads or a gold, silver or leather chain, sometimes containing jewels.

nest

A **nest** is where a bird lays and hatches its eggs. Birds build their nests from sticks and leaves. Other baby animals such as crocodiles, are also born in nests.

newspaper

A **newspaper** is a daily or weekly printed paper which you can read to find out what is going on in the world. Newspapers advertise things and you can find out about radio and television programmes.

nightingale

A **nightingale** is a small, brown bird. Nightingales are well-known for their singing. They are often heard from April to June on warm evenings and sometimes during the day.

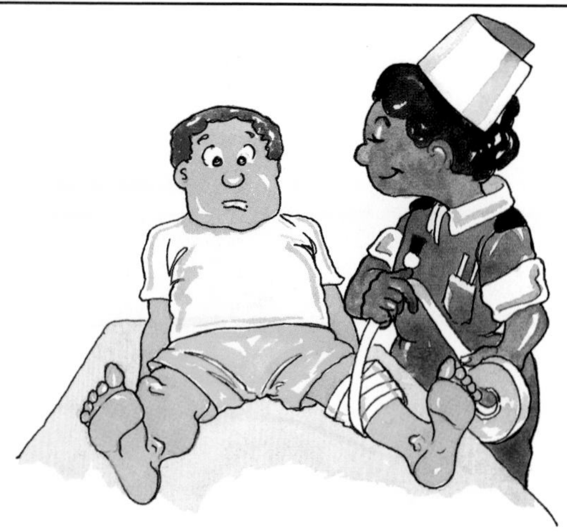

nurse

A **nurse** is a man or woman who looks after sick and injured people in hospital.

O o

oak

An **oak** is a type of tree. The nut of the oak tree is called an acorn. There are 450 different types of oak tree around the world.

oasis

An **oasis** is a place in the desert where there is water. Trees usually grow there.

ocean

An **ocean** is an extremely large area of salt water. Another name for an ocean is the sea. There are four main oceans called the Pacific, Atlantic, Indian and Arctic.

octopus

An **octopus** is a sea creature with a bag-like body and eight long arms called tentacles. The tentacles can be up to 5m long.

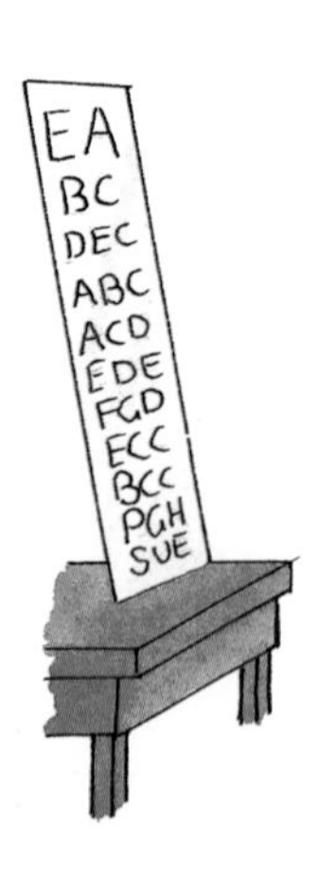

optician

An **optician** is a person who looks after eyes. An optician tests your eyes with special instruments. Opticians make and sell glasses, or spectacles, to help people to see better.

orange

An **orange** is a round, juicy fruit. You remove the peel and eat the segments inside. The colour of an orange is the same as its name.

orchard

An **orchard** is a place where many different types of fruit tree grow. An orchard is usually an enclosed area or part of a garden.

orchestra

An **orchestra** is a group of people who play musical instruments. Orchestras give concerts or provide music for ballets and operas. A conductor stands at the front of an orchestra to keep the musicians in time and tell them when to play loudly and softly.

oyster

An **oyster** is a sea creature that lives inside a pair of shells. Sometimes pearls are found inside oyster shells.

P p

paint

Paint is a thick liquid that comes in many different colours. Paints can be used to colour pictures or to decorate walls.

palace

A **palace** is a large, grand house where a royal family lives. Bishops also live in palaces.

panda

A **panda** is a bear-like mammal found in China. It has black and white fur with large black eye patches. Pandas feed mainly on bamboo. They are rare creatures and very shy. Pandas are closely related to racoons.

park

A **park** is a large garden or area where people can ride bikes, go for walks and play.

parrot

A **parrot** is a bird with brightly-coloured feathers. Some parrots make good pets and can learn to repeat words that are said to them. Parrots come mainly from countries with warm climates and usually live in forests.

peacock

A male peafowl is called a **peacock**. Peacocks are colourful birds with long, brightly patterned tails, which they can spread out like a fan. Peacocks originally come from India and Sri Lanka.

pearl

Pearls are often used to make jewellery, particularly necklaces and earrings. A pearl grows inside the shell of a pearl oyster. Pearls are small and shiny, and can be white or very pale blue in colour.

penguin

A **penguin** is a seabird. Although penguins have wings they cannot fly. They are very good at diving and use their wings and feet to swim.

piano

A **piano** is a large musical instrument. It belongs to the percussion family. Pianos are played by pressing down black and white keys. The keys trigger hammers which hit strings inside the piano and make musical notes.

picnic

A **picnic** is a meal eaten outside. People usually have picnics in the summer when the weather is good.

pier

A **pier** is a long walkway built over the sea. They are very popular in the summer. Some piers have fairground rides and arcades.

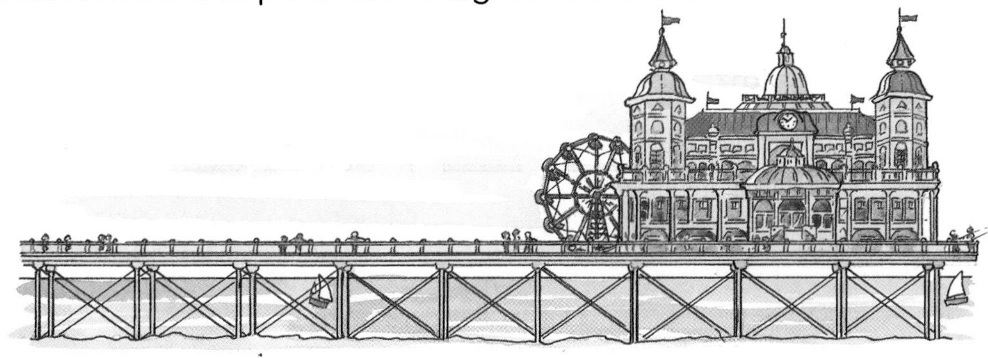

pigeon

A **pigeon** is a very common bird in cities and towns. Pigeons which live in woods and forests are known as wood pigeons. Some people keep pigeons and can train them to fly back home from far away places.

pilot

A **pilot** is a person who has trained very hard to become qualified to fly different types of aircraft.

pirate

Pirates lived a long time ago. They survived by attacking other ships and stealing food and treasure. Many books have been written about pirates. Piracy still exists today.

planet

A **planet** is made of rock, gas, water or ice. We live on the planet Earth which consists of all four. All planets move, or circle, around a large star. The Earth circles the Sun.

playground

A **playground** is a place out of doors where children can play safely. A playground may have rides such as swings, a slide, a roundabout and a see-saw. Schools also have playgrounds where children can play at breaktime.

pumpkin

A **pumpkin** is a very large, round vegetable. It has a hard, pale orange skin. You can carve into pumpkins to make lanterns for Halloween.

puppet

A **puppet** is a doll that can be moved by strings or rods. Another kind of puppet has a body like a glove. You put your hand in and make it move by wiggling your fingers. Sometimes puppets are used in films instead of animals, or as monsters.

pyramids

A **pyramid** is a building, usually found in Egypt, made from blocks of stone. Long ago Egyptians used to bury their kings, known as Pharaohs, inside pyramids.

A **pyramid** shape has a square base and sloping sides that meet in a point at the top.

Q q

quarter

A **quarter** is one of the four equal parts that something can be divided into. It is also written as 1/4.

queen

In some countries, a **queen** is the crowned member of the royal family and the ruler of her country. A queen is also a king's wife when he is ruler of his country.

queue

A **queue** is a line of people or vehicles. People often queue to get on a bus. Cars sometimes have to wait in a queue of traffic.

R r

rabbit

A **rabbit** is a furry animal that digs tunnels under ground to live in. These tunnels lead to the rabbit's warren or burrow. Rabbits have long ears and strong back legs. Tame rabbits can be kept as pets.

radish

A **radish** is a small, hard, red, root vegetable with a peppery taste. Radishes are usually eaten in a salad.

railway

A **railway** is the rail track that trains run on.

rainbow

A **rainbow** is a colourful arc which appears in the sky when the Sun shines through rain. The colours of the rainbow are: red, orange, yellow, green, blue, indigo and violet.

rake

A **rake** is a garden tool with a long handle and a spiked metal bar. Rakes are used for smoothing earth or gravel and clearing up leaves.

raspberries

Raspberries are a soft, red fruit with a sharp taste. They grow on large bushes and are usually ripe in the summer.

refrigerator

A **refrigerator** is a storage place run on electricity where food and drinks are kept cold. The cold temperature keeps the food fresh for longer. A short word for refrigerator is 'fridge'.

reindeer

A **reindeer** is a large deer with antlers. Reindeer usually live in freezing conditions during winter in places such as the North Pole, North America, Greenland and Scandinavia.

reptile

A **reptile** is a cold-blooded animal which usually has dry, scaly skin. Reptiles' young hatch out of eggs. Snakes, lizards and turtles are all reptiles.

rhinoceros

A **rhinoceros** is a large, heavy animal that lives in Africa and Southern Asia. It has a horn on its nose. Rhinos have poor eyesight, but good hearing.

ring

A piece of jewellery worn on the finger is called a **ring**. When people get married they usually exchange rings at the wedding ceremony.

Circle is sometimes another word for **ring**.

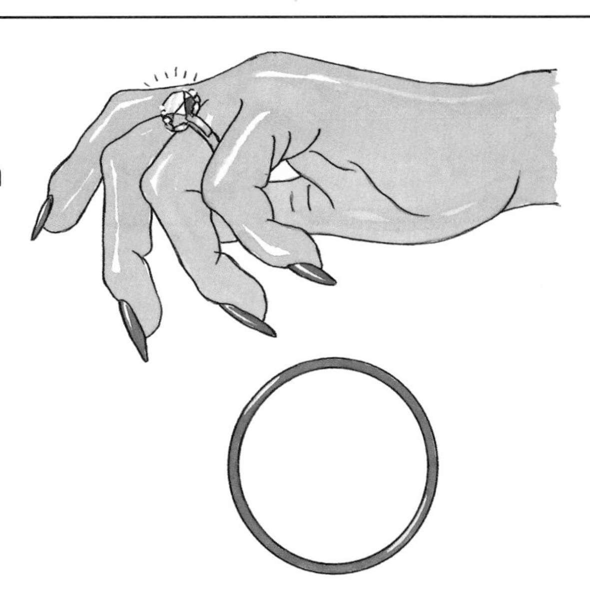

river

A **river** is a large stream of water leading to either the sea or a lake. Fish, ducks and other small creatures live in or by rivers.

robin

A **robin** is a small, brown garden bird with a red breast. Robins live in Europe and are often shown on Christmas cards.

robot

A **robot** is a machine with some human skills. A robot sometimes looks like a human. Robots carry out complicated actions and tasks and are often used in factories where cars are made.

rodeo

A **rodeo** is an exhibition where cowboys show their skills at riding horses. Rodeos are held in parts of America where cowboys use horses to help herd cattle.

rollerblade

Rollerblades are a type of skate. They are boots with a line of wheels attached to the bottom. Rollerblades can be used for fun, or can help you get from place to place quickly.

rocket

A **rocket** is a type of firework that shoots into the sky, making a loud whistling noise and firing out lots of coloured sparks.

Huge **rockets** fire and lift spacecraft into space.

rose

A **rose** is a flower which grows on a prickly bush. Roses come in many colours and usually smell very nice. The stalks of roses have sharp thorns.

Ss

salmon

A **salmon** is a large, silvery-coloured fish. Adult salmon swim back to their birthplace. It is a long, difficult journey because they swim up rivers and leap up waterfalls.

saxophone

A **saxophone** is a long, wind instrument. To play it you blow at the top and press the keys. Saxophones are used mainly to play a type of music called jazz.

scarecrow

A **scarecrow** is a figure made from straw and old clothes. It is placed in a field on a wooden pole to scare birds away from crops.

scarf

A **scarf** is a piece of material worn around the neck. Long, woolly scarves keep you warm in the winter. More delicate scarves can be worn over the shoulders or tied around the head.

scissors

A pair of **scissors** is a tool used for cutting. It has two sharp blades, and two handles to open and close the blades. Scissors come in different sizes, small ones for cutting fingernails, larger ones for cutting hair or material.

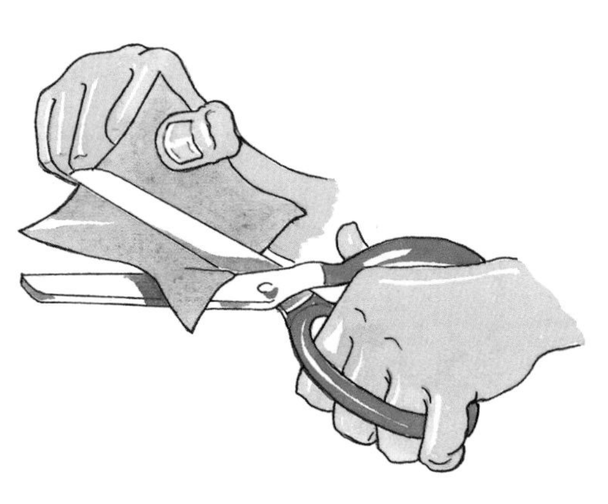

scrapbook

A **scrapbook** is a book of plain paper. You can stick things that are important to you in a scrapbook, such as cuttings, postcards, photographs and pictures.

shadow

A **shadow** is the black shape made when light falls onto a person or object. Shadows only show the solid outline of a shape

shark

A **shark** is a large, fierce fish with lots of sharp, pointed teeth. Sharks have a large fin on their back. This is called a dorsal fin.

sheep

A **sheep** is an animal with a thick, woolly coat. Sheep usually stay in flocks and live in fields. A sheep's coat is cut off and the fleece is spun into wool.

ship

A **ship** is a large boat that makes long journeys over the sea. There are many different types of ship. A passenger ship carries people and a cargo ship transports goods.

shoe

A **shoe** is a strong leather or plastic covering that protects the feet. Shoes have strong soles and do not come above the ankle.

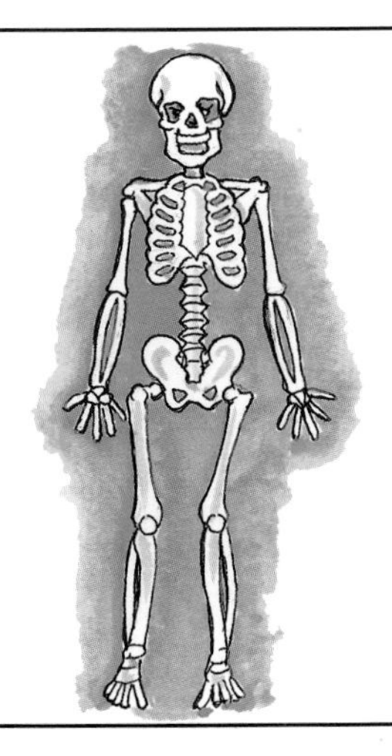

skeleton

The **skeleton** is the framework of bones inside your body. Skeletons protect our inside organs. An adult skeleton usually has 206 bones.

ski

To **ski** is to move over snow on two long, thin pieces of wood or plastic which are fixed to your feet. You hold long poles to give you balance. Skiing was invented 5000 years ago as a means of transport.

slug

A **slug** is a small creature found mostly in gardens. Slugs are covered in slime which helps them to move. Slugs prefer to stay in damp places and mainly come out at night to eat plants.

smile

To **smile** is to turn up the corners of your mouth. You smile to show that you are happy or pleased.

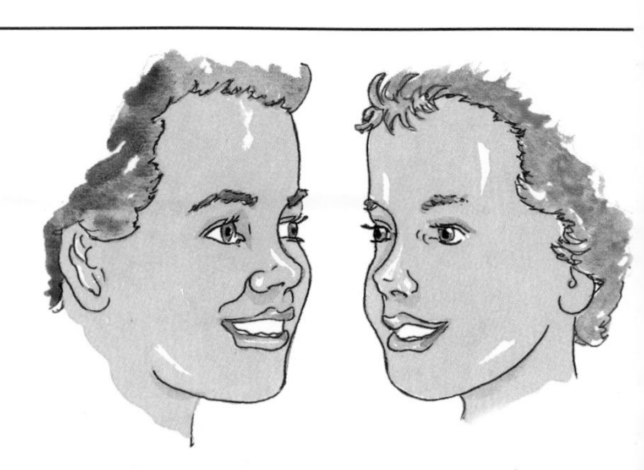

snail

A **snail** is a small, slow-moving creature. Snails have a hard spiral shell which they carry on their backs. Common snails live in gardens whilst others live in ponds or the sea.

snake

A **snake** is a long, limbless reptile with dry, scaly skin. There are many different types of snake, some of which can be very poisonous and deadly. They usually have forked tongues which they use to smell.

snow

Frozen water that falls from the sky as light, white flakes is called **snow**. Snow falls in the winter when the weather is cold.

spaghetti

Spaghetti is a type of pasta, which comes in long strands. When it is cooked it looks like soft string. Spaghetti, eaten with a sauce, is an Italian meal.

spider

A **spider** is a creature with eight legs. Some spiders spin webs to catch their food. Spiders can come in different sizes, but most of them are quite small.

spire

A **spire** is the tall, pointed top of a church tower. Long ago, a spire made it easier for people to find their way to church, as the spire could be seen from far away.

stable

A **stable** is a building where horses are kept. Stable doors are in two halves so that the top can be left open and the horses can look out when they are shut in the stable.

star

A **star** is the light seen in the night sky. Stars are made from dust and gas in space. The Sun is one of the largest stars in our galaxy.

Star is also the word used for the shape which has five or six points.

statue

A **statue** is a model of an important person or animal. Statues are usually carved or moulded out of wood, stone or metal.

strawberry

A **strawberry** is a soft, pinkish-red fruit with a covering of small seeds. Strawberries are very sweet and usually eaten with cream.

submarine

A **submarine** is a ship that travels under water.

sun

The **Sun** gives the Earth light during the day. When the Sun shines you feel warm. The Sun rises early in the morning in the East and sets in the evening in the West.

swan

A **swan** is a large bird which has white feathers, an orange beak and webbed feet. There are also black swans with red beaks which live mostly in Australia. Swans swim in ponds and lakes and can fly long distances.

swim

To **swim** means to move in water. We swim by moving our arms and legs. Many animals can swim.

T t

tambourine

A **tambourine** is a percussion instrument. It is like a small drum that you hold in your hands with small cymbals slotted around. You shake a tambourine or hit it with your fingers to make music.

teacher

A **teacher** is a person who helps people to learn different subjects. Children and adults have teachers at school and college.

teeth

Teeth are the small, hard, white parts which grow in your gums inside your mouth. You use your teeth to chew food. It is very important to brush your teeth to keep them clean and healthy.

telephone

A **telephone** is an instrument that carries sound from one place to another. We use telephones to speak to each other. Many people carry mobile telephones which can be used almost anywhere.

telescope

A **telescope** is a tube with a lens at each end. When you look through a telescope it makes things far away seem closer. On a clear night people use telescopes to look at the stars.

tennis

A game of **tennis** is played on a court with a net across the middle. Players use rackets to hit a ball over the net to the players on the other side of the court.

theatre

A **theatre** is a large building or outdoor area with a stage where actors, entertainers and dancers perform shows to an audience.

thermometer

A **thermometer** is a long, thin instrument with numbers to show how hot or cold something is. You have your temperature taken with a thermometer when you are ill.

throne

A **throne** is a large, grand seat raised on a higher level for a king, queen, pope or bishop. Thrones are used for ceremonies or other important occasions.

tiger

A **tiger** is a large, wild animal and is a member of the cat family. Tigers have orange or white fur with black stripes and live in the forests and jungles of Asia.

toad

A **toad** is a creature with a rough, dry skin. Toads look like frogs but are usually larger. Toads live mainly on land but also spend a lot of time in water.

tongue

The **tongue** forms part of the mouth. People use their tongues to taste, lick, swallow and speak. Many animals use their tongues to clean themselves, especially cats and dogs. Snakes smell with their tongues.

tortoise

A **tortoise** is a slow-moving reptile that has a hard shell on its back. Tortoises live in dry and warm countries, such as Africa.

tractor

A **tractor** is a large machine used on farms. It has big wheels and can pull heavy loads.

train

A **train** is an engine that pulls carriages. It travels along railway tracks to get people or goods to different places.

trampoline

A **trampoline** is a large piece of canvas joined to a metal frame by springs. You can have a lot of fun jumping and bouncing on a trampoline.

trumpet

A **trumpet** is a brass musical instrument. When you blow through it and press the keys you can make musical notes. Trumpets are played mainly in brass bands.

twins

Twins are two people or animals born at the same time. Some twins look so much alike that it is difficult to tell which is which – they are called identical twins. Others don't look alike at all.

U u

umbrella

An **umbrella** is made of waterproof cloth stretched over a metal frame and is attached to a long stick with a handle. When it is opened an umbrella keeps you dry in the rain.

unicorn

A **unicorn** is a mythical animal that looks like a white horse, but has a straight horn sticking out from the top of its head.

uniform

A **uniform** is a type of clothing worn by people to show that they are part of the same group. A uniform is also worn to show the different jobs that people do, for example firemen.

V v

valley

A **valley** is the low land that lies between hills or mountains. Valleys often have a river or stream running through the middle.

vegetable

A **vegetable** is a plant that can be eaten. Most vegetables need to be peeled and cooked, but some are good to eat raw.

vet

A **vet** is a person who looks after and treats sick or injured animals. The word vet is short for veterinarian. People take their pet to a veterinary surgery when the animal is sick.

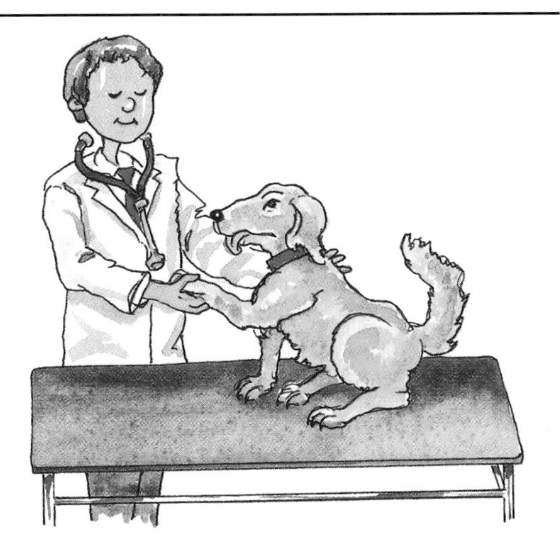

village

A **village** is made up of a small number of houses and other buildings such as a church and school. Villages are usually in the countryside and are smaller than towns and cities.

violin

A **violin** is a musical instrument belonging to the string family. Violins have four strings and are played with a bow made out of wood and horsehair. Violins are mostly played in an orchestra.

volcano

A **volcano** is a mountain that contains hot liquid, gas and ash. Sometimes volcanoes erupt and hot lava bursts out of the crater at the top.

W w

walrus

A **walrus** is a type of seal with long tusks. Walruses live in icy waters in the Arctic Circle. These creatures grow a thick layer of fat, called blubber, to keep them warm.

wasp

A **wasp** is a small flying insect with a yellow and black body. When wasps are disturbed they can sting you.

weasel

A **weasel** is a small, brown and white furry animal with a long body. Weasels usually live in the woodlands of Europe, Asia and North Africa.

wedding

The ceremony between a man and woman when they get married is called a **wedding**. At the wedding the bride and groom promise to stay together for the rest of their lives.

whale

A **whale** is a large mammal that lives in the sea. The Blue Whale is the largest mammal in the world.

wheel

A **wheel** is a round object which can turn. Wheels can be found on most vehicles to make them move.

windmill

A **windmill** is a building with four large blades, or sails, connected to its outside. When the wind blows, the blades move and make the machinery inside work. Years ago windmills were used to grind grain and turn it into flour. There are not many working windmills now.

wing

A **wing** is the part of a bird, insect or aircraft that enables it to fly. Birds and insects flap or beat their wings to fly. Most aircraft have engines under the wings to lift them off the ground.

worm

A **worm** is a long, thin creature that burrows in the soil. Earthworms are helpful to gardeners as they help to make the soil more fertile.

x-ray

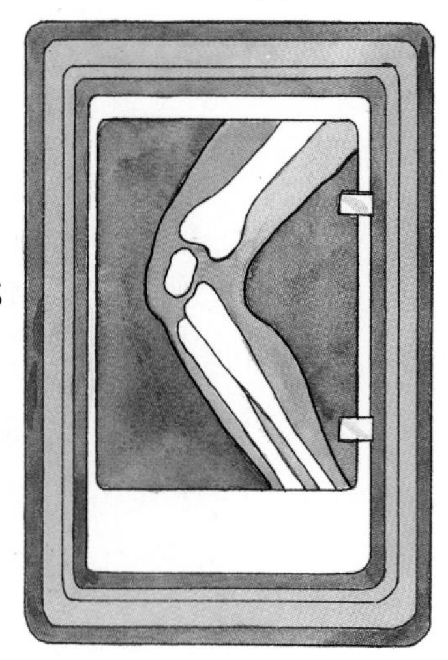

An **x-ray** is a photographic plate taken by a special machine that shows the bones and insides of the body. The photographs show any fractures or infections. They will also show objects which may have accidentally been swallowed.

xylophone

A **xylophone** is a musical instrument belonging to the percussion family. It has a row of metal bars that are hit with small hammers to make different musical notes.

Y y

yacht

A **yacht** is a light sailing boat. It has sails made of strong material which catch the wind and make it move across the water. This type of yacht is often used for racing. Larger yachts often have an engine.

yoghurt

Yoghurt is a food made from soured milk. Sometimes it is sold with fruit mixed into it. Yoghurt is usually eaten as a snack or as a healthy dessert.

yolk

The **yolk** is the yellow part of an egg. When you cut open a boiled egg you can see the yolk and the white parts. Sometimes, the uncooked yolk and egg-white are mixed together and used in cooking.

Z z

zebra

A **zebra** is a wild animal found in Africa. Zebras look like horses but their bodies are marked with black and white stripes.

zip

A **zip** is a fastener with metal or plastic teeth that join two edges of material together. Zips are used instead of buttons on some clothes. They are also used on luggage.

zoo

A **zoo** is a place where animals from all over the world are kept. Zoos look after endangered creatures, and people can go and see them to learn more about them.